A Workbook for *Outlive*

Practical Applications of Effective Life Advice

Bianca Wolf

© Copyright 2023 by Bianca Wolf. All rights reserved.

The materials comprising the literary work presented herein have been produced for entertainment and informational intent. The content creator(s) have carried out every possible effort to ensure the contents' accuracy and veracity. Notwithstanding, the content creator(s) do not claim to be experts on the subject matter or purport unquestionable validity. Consequently, readers must conduct research to verify the contents' accuracy while seeking whatever professional counsel they deem appropriate.

This copyright statement declares a legally binding contract as determined by the Committee of Publishers Association as well as the American Bar Association within the jurisdiction pertaining to the United States of America. Applicable legislation shall govern copyright issues in jurisdictions outside of the United States. No portion of the contents contained herein shall be reproduced, broadcast, or disseminated, in any form, without the copyright holder's consent. Any unauthorized use of this literary work's contents shall be deemed copyright infringement and subject to the appropriate legal claims as allowed by American copyright legislation.

The information, descriptions, events, or any other data contained in this literary work have been determined to be true and fair. Nevertheless, the accounts in this literary work are not deemed true in the case of a literary work of fiction. Thus, the creator(s) and publisher are exempt from any responsibility of actions stemming from the reader's own accord. Advice, recommendations, tips, or techniques are not to be construed as giving professional advice. The reader must seek appropriate professional counsel before putting any of the information contained forthwith into practice.

Table of Contents

Introduction and Disclaimer.......................6
   Disclaimer 7
Chapter 1: Nutrition 8
   Macronutrients.......................................9
      Carbohydrates 10
      Proteins..12
      Fats 14
      Water...15
   Micronutrients 17
      Vitamins 19
      Minerals 24
      Trace Elements............................27
      Conclusion of Micronutrients 31
      Calories..32
Chapter 2: Exercise 34
   Different Forms of Exercise 35
Chapter 3: Sleep....................................41
   The Stages of Sleep............................. 41
   Deprivation..46
Chapter 4: Mental Health 49
   Cultivating a Peaceful Mind................49
   Specific Mental illnesses 54

Depression *54*
Anxiety *57*
Bipolar Disorder *60*
Conclusion on Disorders *63*
Chapter 5: Chronic Illnesses..................... **64**
Chronic Illnesses of the Mind 64
Dementia *64*
Chronic Organ Illnesses 69
Chronic Bone and Nervous Illnesses 72
Conclusion **77**

Introduction and Disclaimer

Peter Attia is a physician, longevity expert, and entrepreneur. He is the founder and CEO of the company Attia Medical, a practice and company that focuses on helping improve people's health and longevity through individual plans for nutrition, exercise, and general lifestyles.

As a health expert, Attia was constantly considering how one could optimize their health. As a researcher, he extended that consideration and approached it empirically. Eventually, Attia's life's work and research culminated in his book, *Outlive*. *Outlive* is a book detailing exactly how one might live for as long as one can. Most notably, the book covers how one should maintain their diet, exercise habits, sleep schedule, and mental health, and finally, it explains different chronic illnesses, their prevention, and their treatment.

Receiving advice is one thing. It's nice to read a book and then think about it for a while before continuing on with your life. Applying that advice, however, is a whole different story. It takes time and commitment to fully create a new habit. This process of creating a habit is exactly what this book will help you with. Not only will we encourage you to start a good habit, but this book is written so that those habits will last!

Disclaimer

This workbook is only referential to *Outlive* by Peter Attia. This work is not meant, in any way, to substitute *Outlive* or other works for that matter. The advice that this workbook alludes to is well-established and acknowledged far beyond any works of Attia.

The knowledge that this workbook provides is general advice. Following the advice in this workbook does not guarantee a specific effect for every individual. The advice in this book is true and good for *most* people, not *every* person. Follow the advice of this book at your own risk.

The advice in this book regarding mental health is limited to the general consensus and suggestions that are made for most people. If you are struggling with severe mental illness, the only solution is a licensed medical professional.

Chapter 1: Nutrition

One of the most foundational and talked about concepts in all of health is nutrition. Are you eating too much? Are you not eating enough? Are you eating the right things, regardless of the amount? Trying to answer all these questions is, no doubt, exhausting and overwhelming.

Furthermore, nutrition is subjective. The right diet for each person depends on that person's level of activity, age, sex, and even just how their digestive system works!

Because of the subjectivity of the concept, it's also very controversial. Hardcore diet plans are known to be detrimental to people's mental health, but many still champion them. Simple and modern diets (e.g., Keto) work sometimes, but even when they do, they're known to have drawbacks (Keto, for example, is known to increase cholesterol and risk of heart disease for certain people). Furthermore, many people diet unnecessarily, which can cause hormonal shifts, mood swings, and a variety of other health issues.

The point is: There's no perfect diet for everyone. The best piece of advice for healthy eating (diet or not) is just to be conscious of the food that you're eating and its effects. Achieving that dietary consciousness is the exact goal of this book. Throughout the following chapter, we're going to explain the foundations of nutrition and have you do some exercises that will help you understand exactly what your diet is doing for you.

Macronutrients

Macronutrients are the nutrients that we need to eat consistently and in large amounts in order to sustain ourselves. Macronutrients include carbohydrates, proteins, fats, cholesterol, fiber, and water. Many will hesitate to think of water as a nutrient, but we're certain that you'll understand the importance of hydration by the end of this chapter. Macronutrients are needed on a daily basis, or there will be consequences to your health (especially in carbs and protein, as they are your main source of energy).

Carbohydrates

Carbohydrates, or "carbs" for short, are the main source of energy in your body. Carbs are split up into three categories: sugars, starches, and fiber.

Sugars are simple carbohydrates that burn up in your body quickly. That means that when you eat sugar, it will give you energy quickly, but it won't last very long— hence the concept of sugar highs and sugar crashes.

Starch is a specific polymeric carbohydrate. It is the carb that is in bread and beans.

Finally, fiber. Though fiber is technically a starch, it's usually put into its own category because of its unique properties. Fiber is especially hard for us to digest, so it's not considered to be a source of energy. However, fiber is very important. Dietary fiber helps exercise your digestive tract, balance out acids, and adds bulk to your meals, which makes them more satisfying.

When talking about carbs, we usually mean starch. Sugar has its own unique uses, and fiber doesn't have the same nutritional value.

The CDC doesn't recommend any amount of carbs based on weight, age, height, or any other metric that would affect how carbs are absorbed— they explain that the answer is too complicated for any website to try and give a group of people. The CDC does, however, insist on eating meals that have consistent amounts of carbs throughout the day so that your blood sugar doesn't spike or drop suddenly (which would negatively affect your mood).

To help you understand how your meals are balanced and how many carbs you eat, we've constructed this table. On top of three meals a day, many nutritionists will insist that a little snack in between meals helps prevent overeating or mood swings, so we've included portions for those snacks, as well.

Nutritional information can be found on the packaging of all of your foods and ingredients. If you decide to eat fast food, their nutritional information can be found online. Make sure to add up all of the ingredients used in preparing your meals; Don't just write down the carbs of the main ingredient (e.g., the chicken in Chicken Parmesan).

Meal	Carbs
Carbs consumed for breakfast	
Snack between breakfast and lunch	
Carbs consumed for lunch	
Snack between lunch and dinner	
Carbs consumed for dinner	

Tracking your carb intake throughout the day should be your first step in changing your diet for the better; it will also likely be the one with the greatest effect.

Beyond just the next day (we advise you to track and log things as soon as you hear the advice for them), it is a good idea to consistently log your carbs. Consistency is the only way to create a habit— good or bad!

Proteins

Whenever it comes to exercising, you hear a lot of things about protein. Protein is a reasonable thing to talk about so much because it is the building block for just about everything in your body! That includes muscle, so when you're exercising and trying to gain muscle mass, you need to eat enough protein to build it up!

Furthermore, if you already have a lot of muscle mass, you need to keep eating protein so that you can sustain it and avoid injuries. That is just one of many reasons that protein is so important.

Beyond support, proteins are one of only three macronutrients that you can get calories from, which means that lacking protein in your diet means that you might be lacking vital, healthy energy!

To know how many grams of protein you should eat on a daily basis, you're going to need to do some math. The Mayo Clinic recommends that you should eat .8 grams of protein for every kilogram that you weigh. This suggestion, however, is for "sedentary" adults, meaning that you will likely need more protein in order to prevent injury and continue to develop muscle. People who exercise regularly should get 1.1-1.5 grams of protein per kilogram that they weigh.

Use the equation for pounds to kilograms () and then multiply by the amount of recommended protein that suits you. In the following table, fill out how much protein you eat on a daily basis and then compare to it the amount of protein you need.

Total amount of protein consumed in one day	g
Amount of protein recommended for one day	g
Difference between recommended and consumed protein	g

How much more protein do you need? What do you think are good and bad sources of this protein? Many athletes consume protein powder or other supplements in order to make sure they meet the recommended amount, but that method generally isn't recommended for people who don't work out due to the fact that the lack of protein likely indicates a lack of other necessary nutrients.

Fats

Fats are probably the most misunderstood nutrient. In many ways, fat is good! Fats (or lipids, as many dieticians will call them, though there *is* a difference) are actually necessary. If you don't consume enough alpha-linolenic (omega-3) and linoleic (omega-6), which are both compounds of fatty acids, then you will cultivate a deficiency!

Fats carry nutrients in your bloodstream, help support the connective tissue between your muscles, and help maintain healthy skin and hair! But don't let this praise fool you; there are definitely some problems with eating many fats.

Trans fats, for one, are made by the addition of hydrogen molecules to a once-healthy vegetable oil. These fats, more than anything, are to be avoided. They raise low-density-lipoprotein (LDL) cholesterol, which is very unhealthy, and lower high-density-lipoprotein (HDH), in which case, higher is better. Trans fats can be found naturally, but they're most common in processed foods, so eating natural and "raw" can help reduce the risk of high cholesterol and heart disease.

Tracking fats is a notably difficult task. Instead, we are just going to work on being more conscious of the kinds of fats we're eating. Below, please list five different kinds of fats that you ate in the past 24 hours (most of this information can be found in a simple Google search):

Type of Fat	Is it healthy or unhealthy?

Overall, simply knowing things like how avocados have the good kind of fat helps prevent the misconception that you should avoid fat altogether.

Water

Water is the most important nutrient. Without carbs or protein, you could last a while (up to two months, assuming you are well prepared), but without water, you have three days. Considering how little time you would last without water, it's hard to imagine that being dehydrated wouldn't come with long-term consequences to your health.

Water averages about 60% of your body weight; it helps you regulate your temperature, lubricate your joints, digest your food, and acts as a solvent to get rid of waste— it even keeps your skin looking healthy!

Though water seems like something that should be consumed in abundance, there are drawbacks to overconsumption. Your kidneys, depending on your height, weight, and sex, can filter .7-1 liter of water per hour. Consuming beyond that amount can result in acute water toxicity. To maintain a healthy intake, the National Institute of Medicine recommends 3.7L of water for men and 2.7 for women.

When you're drinking water, we'd like for you to read the small print that details how many fluid ounces are in the container and log them. After logging the amount for the day, continue doing so for a full week! While looking at the days you are more or less hydrated, think about the ways that situation was caused and how to prevent/induce them.

Day	Fl Oz consumed

What is the average amount of water that you consumed in a day? How can you make that amount more ideal, and what's preventing that from happening?

Micronutrients

Micronutrients are nutrients that do not need to be consumed as frequently or in as large amounts as things like macronutrients. Micronutrients are needed for things like your metabolism and child growth and development. Generally, micronutrients are especially necessary when you're sick or young enough that your body is still not fully developed. There are three categories of micronutrients: vitamins, minerals, and trace elements.

Minerals are inorganic. The body uses minerals for various functions, such as building strong bones and teeth, regulating muscle function, and balancing out fluid.

Trace elements are minerals that are needed in very small amounts. Though not necessary in large amounts, our body still needs them to function!

There are two kinds of vitamins. These are fat and water solubility. Fat-soluble vitamins can become unhealthy if you eat too much before your body is able to digest them. Water-soluble vitamins must be consumed every day.

Not having enough micronutrients can cause a bunch of health issues, such as anemia, a weakened immune system, impaired vision, and reduced growth in young people. It is important to consume a diet that includes all parts of the food pyramid and groups to be sure that you're eating enough of all your micronutrients. In some cases, dietary supplements may be necessary to ensure sufficient intake of certain micronutrients, especially for individuals with specific health conditions or dietary restrictions. Dietary supplements for older people are especially common.

Vitamins

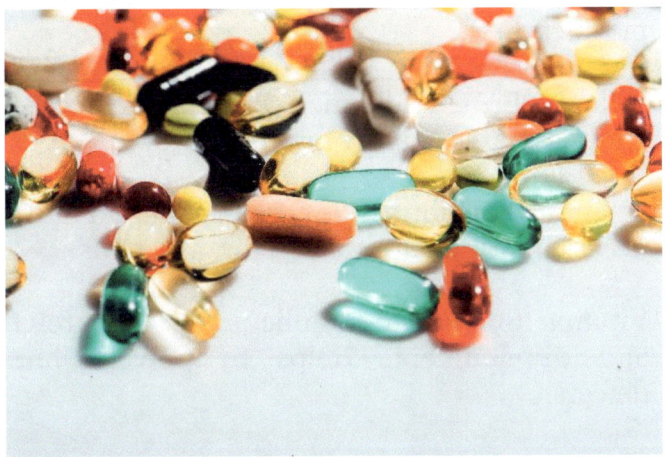

Vitamins are essential. They help maintain your health and prevent diseases. Your body needs a total of about 13 vitamins, and each vitamin has a specific role to play in the body.

The 13 necessary vitamins and their uses are as follows:

Vitamin B1 (Thiamine): Energy production and nerve function.

Vitamin B2 (Riboflavin): Healthy skin and eyes, energy production.

Vitamin B3 (Niacin): Digestion and helps with healthy skin, nerves, and helps with energy production.

Vitamin B5 (Pantothenic acid): Helps to maintain healthy skin, hair, and eyes. Energy production.

Vitamin B6 (Pyridoxine): Protein metabolism and maintains healthy brain function.

Vitamin B7 (Biotin): Energy production and is necessary for healthy skin, hair, and nails.

Vitamin B9 (Folate or folic acid): Cell growth and development. Helps to prevent birth defects.

Vitamin B12 (Cobalamin): Keeping your nerves healthy and working while replenishing red blood cells.

Vitamin A: Vision, immune function, and skin health.

Vitamin C: Immune system and helps with wound healing.

Vitamin D: Aides in absorbing calcium.

Vitamin E: Protects body/cells against harm caused by "free radicals."

Vitamin K: Prevents clotting and promotes health.

Vitamins are important for many reasons, some of which are as follows:

Vitamins are involved in many bodily processes, including metabolism, immune function, and energy production.

B vitamins improve mood and reduce *symptoms* of depression. Though, of course, depression is too nuanced of an illness to assume to be solved by eating enough vitamins.

Vitamin E and vitamin C help maintain healthy skin. They defend your skin from harm from "free radicals" and help with collagen production.

Vitamins are also important for maintaining healthy vision. For example, vitamin A is essential for good vision, and a deficiency in this vitamin can lead to night blindness.

Now that we understand the importance of vitamins, let's discuss some recommendations on how to get enough vitamins in your diet.

The best way to get enough vitamins is to maintain a diet that has something from each of the main food groups.

Many foods are nutrient-dense, which means that they have a higher number of vitamins and minerals per gram.

Despite common misconceptions, the sun doesn't give you vitamin D; your body is just less inhibited while producing vitamin D when you are outside enough. Getting enough sunlight can help to ensure that your body has enough vitamin D.

Sometimes, when you cook food, it breaks down or burns up vitamins. Consider cooking your food in ways that preserve vitamins better, such as steaming or roasting.

Tracking your vitamins is difficult. Knowing the exact amount is even harder. So, we've created a chart that is meant for you to understand the kinds of vitamins that you receive on a daily basis so that you can at least understand what you are and aren't getting!

Day	Mon	Tues	Wed	Thurs	Fri	Sat	Sun
Vit							

Don't be convinced that you must start on Monday! Start on the more recent day that you can recall what you ate and just go all the way around the week. After you fill out the table for the week, review this section and think about what vitamins you did and didn't get. How do you think you can get them? (Make sure that this method will work consistently for a long time—something like learning a new recipe won't always do!) What method mentioned in this section did you use?

Minerals

Minerals are inorganic, and you need them in order to keep your digestive processes functioning. These actions that need minerals in order to be carried out are: regulating your fluids, bones, and teeth, as well as nerve and muscle function. Unlike many vitamins, the body can't produce minerals, so they have to be consumed in order to prevent deficiency. We've listed the most important minerals, which are also the ones that your body needs to function! Deficiencies in these minerals can lead to serious health problems, including brittle bones, anemia, and a damaged immune system.

Calcium is essential for bone health and is necessary for muscle health and nerve strength. Calcium's found all over— not just in milk— there are also leafy vegetables as well as nuts and seeds if you're feeling like a squirrel. Despite its abundance, many people do not consume enough calcium on a daily or weekly basis. To prevent calcium deficiency, you should consume at least three servings of calcium foods per day.

Iron is one of a few crucial ingredients in your blood cells! A deficiency can lead to anemia, which furthermore, causes fatigue and a poor immune system, which can bring about even worse issues! Iron can be found in both plant and animal-based foods! A fun fact about iron-based foods (that *is* a little gross): if you blend them up and their iron content is high enough, you can use a magnet to fish out the little bits of iron! But anyways, to ensure adequate iron intake, individuals should consume at least one iron-rich food per day.

Zinc is a crucial mineral. Though it is also considered a trace element, it's important enough that many consider it a mineral (which is differentiated by how much one needs to consume) because it is so important for immune function, wound healing, and the creation of new DNA. It is all over, specifically in beef (and other red meats), beans, and nuts. Despite this apparent abundance, just like iron, a lot of people don't eat it enough and face the consequences! To prevent a zinc deficiency, individuals should consume at least one serving of zinc-rich food per day.

Magnesium is also important for muscle and nerve function. Magnesium is also necessary in order for you to maintain healthy bones. You can find magnesium in plenty of different foods, especially whole grains, and nuts! Leafy greens are also generally a good source of minerals. Just like the other minerals, you should eat at least one serving of magnesium-rich foods daily. You need potassium for a range of things. Nervous function and muscle health are the main concerns, but your body will also have trouble balancing your fluids if it doesn't have enough potassium (which would make it harder for you to process water and stay hydrated). We all know there is potassium in bananas, but it's also abundant in potatoes. Leafy greens are a universal go-to, and potassium is, once again, not an exception! To prevent potassium deficiency, you should consume at least one serving of potassium-rich food per day.

Sodium is a controversial mineral. Your body needs sodium for nervous health and fluid balance, but consuming too much sodium is often bad for your blood pressure and heart. While trying to ward off a deficiency, your consumption of sodium shouldn't exceed 2,300 milligrams daily, which is the recommended daily intake for adults, according to the CDC. An overconsumption of sodium can be harmful to your heart health and cholesterol. Frequently eating fast food is one of the best-known ways that people overconsume sodium and fats, which often leads to severe heart issues.

Over the next day, try to think about how much sodium you've eaten. Fill in the amount below:

Is that amount more or less than the recommended amount? Higher sodium is often dangerous, but a significantly lower amount can be even worse for many people!

Now fill out the different minerals that you've eaten in the past three days. If you can, estimate the amount of each mineral to the nearest milligram.

Mineral	Amount
Zinc	
Magnesium	
Potassium	
Iron	
Sodium	

Consult the chart and the recommendations to ensure that you're eating around the correct amount of each mineral. Also, reread this previous section to understand how important it is that you meet the recommendation for each mineral. Number the minerals 1-6 by how important you think it is that you meet the requirements based on the information above.

Trace Elements

Trace elements are nutrients that the body needs in very small quantities to perform important functions. They're known as "trace elements" because they are only needed in small amounts compared to other micronutrients. Most of these elements are technically minerals, but they're also usually metals and in a pure, elemental (as in you can find them on the periodic table) form.

Copper is a trace element that is used to make red blood cells and build up your bones. Your immune system is also sustained by copper! It's a big deal. Copper is found in a variety of foods, including the usual nuts and whole grains, but it is also abundant in the liver. To make sure that you get enough copper, you should make sure to eat at least one of those (or other copper-abundant foods) daily!

Iodine is another trace element. It's important for thyroid function and producing thyroid hormones. You can find iodine in seafood, but also dairy, and, of course, iodized salt. Iodine is another one of those micronutrients that are known for deficiencies! Many people don't have enough iodine in their diets. To prevent iodine deficiency, you should make sure to eat seafood frequently (for vegetarians, this does include seaweed, which is a great snack!).

Selenium is important for immune and thyroid function. Selenium also helps build up and strengthen your nails, skin, and hair! You can find selenium all over! When looking for selenium, think "things connected to the earth." So, leafy greens, which come out of the ground, as well as root vegetables. Seafood also has a lot of selenium. To prevent a selenium deficiency, you should include foods that you know have a reasonable amount of this trace element at least once a day.

Chromium is important for insulin and blood sugar control. You can find chromium in many foods, especially ones that are grown in the Earth in areas with high chromium. To prevent a deficiency, you should consume at least one serving of food that's rich in chromium daily.

Manganese is a trace element that is specifically known for bone health. Wound healing and the ability to digest carbohydrates are also known benefits. Furthermore, manganese helps your body break down amino acids and cholesterol, which can help build muscle and prevent obesity (though it would be a ridiculous idea that one could just quickly lose weight because of manganese). Manganese is found in the usual foods for trace elements: whole grain. In order to keep yourself from reaching a deficiency in manganese, please make sure that you're consuming a food that has a notable amount of manganese on a daily basis.

Zinc is also considered a trace element, but it is better known as a mineral. Considering that fact and the fact that this micronutrient has already been covered, we've decided to omit zinc from this section.

While reading this, you might have noticed common foods that are rich in each of these micronutrients. That does not mean that you should just eat a bunch of nuts and expect yourself to never have another nutritional problem. The real answer to finding all of these micronutrients is a good, varied diet as well as a consciousness of the benefits and shortcomings of the different foods that you are eating.

If your diet is deficient in a variety of micronutrients and you don't have the means of changing it (e.g., you're unable to afford different, organic foods consistently), then supplements might be the answer. With supplements, you can identify what nutrient you're coming up short on and take a pill for it once a day or even once a week! (depending on the nutrient and the dosage).

When thinking about trace elements, it's important to know that they are needed in smaller amounts than most. Please read the nutrition labels to make sure you are getting enough of each element. Write an X to the right of each box if, in the past three days, you've consumed enough of each trace element:

Trace Element	X
Chromium	
Iodine	
Copper	
Selenium	

Conclusion of Micronutrients

Though the word "micro" is in micronutrients, they're no small matter! The information on the micronutrients is a lot to take in, so we recommend slowly rereading this section to understand everything fully. Furthermore, applying this knowledge to the real world is the best way to solidify it. So, we've made a set of questions to quiz you about what is in each food. Do your own research to fill out the different kinds of micronutrients that are in each of these meals:

Hamburger and fries:

    Vitamin:

    Mineral:

    Trace Element:

Spaghetti and red sauce:

    Vitamin:

    Mineral:

    Trace Element:

Red Velvet Cake:

    Vitamin:

Mineral:

Trace Element:

Calories

Many people assume that calories are a specific macro- or micro-nutrient. That is not the case. Calories are a unit of measurement used to demonstrate the energy content of the food you're eating. Calories represent how much energy a gram of water needs to be raised by a single degree Celsius. In nutrition, we use calories to show how much energy we get from a serving of food (or drink, in many cases).

When we eat and drink, we digest the molecules. The molecules are broken down into their most basic parts (e.g., when we eat bread, we break it down into carbs for energy). The carbs or protein are used, then, as fuel in our bodies to do things like write a book or read that book and take its advice. The amount of energy that our cells can extract from these molecules is measured in calories.

Estimating caloric intake begins with understanding that not all food carries the same amount of energy within it. When compared with protein or carbs, fats contain a higher number of calories per gram consumed, thus making them denser, calorically speaking. That is why foods like cheese or fried snacks that fall under this category tend to be higher in caloric density when compared with nutritionally balanced options like fruits and vegetables.

When you consume calories, they're expected to become energy. If they don't become energy, then they just sit there. But bread (to continue our example) won't last in your body. So, in order to preserve that energy, our body stores the leftover carbs as fat in our bodies. Therefore, consuming too many calories can lead to weight gain, and consuming too few will lead to weight loss since that excess fat will be burned. A balanced diet can help you to maintain a healthy calorie balance. Meeting the recommended amount from the USDA helps you sustain a healthy body.

Chapter 2: Exercise

Exercise, after nutrition, might be one of the most confusing topics in this book. Exercise raises a lot of questions, like: How can/should I lose weight while exercising, or what is the best way to build strength, or how often should I exercise?

Staying active is essential for staying healthy, but how much physical activity should you be aiming for? Depending on your individual needs and fitness level, the American Heart Association suggests getting a minimum of two hours and thirty minutes of moderate exercise or an hour and fifteen minutes of vigorous exercise weekly.

For optimal results and a well-rounded fitness routine, two days per week dedicated to strength training exercises targeting major muscle groups is also recommended.

Don't think that these recommendations are absolute and final facts on the topic of exercise. The necessary amount of exercise to maintain and cultivate a healthy body varies tremendously by sex, age, height, gender, and diet! The only people that could truly understand what is needed are yourself and a licensed nutritionist!

Beyond exercise frequency, it's crucial to take into account the intensity and duration of your workouts, as well as any rest and recovery periods necessary. Experts generally suggest beginning with low intensity and gradually increasing it so as to prevent injury and encourage ongoing advancement. This is generally known as progressive overload.

Generally, to burn weight, it's a good idea to simply elevate your heart rate above its resting rate for a substantial amount of time. Walking is a wonderful method. Even top athletes will simply walk around on their lower-impact days!

Different Forms of Exercise

People frequently debate what the best form of exercise is, but the answer varies greatly on what someone is trying to achieve and who they are. There are three different exercises that are known to improve people's quality of life: HIIT, cardio, and weightlifting.

Cardio, HIIT (high-intensity interval training), and weightlifting are the most popular forms of exercise. Though HIIT is technically a form of weightlifting, it uses a special system that clearly separates it from the category. Let's look at each of these exercises individually.

Cardio, short for cardiovascular exercise, is technically any form of exercise that consistently raises your heart rate above its resting level, but it's really seen as a continuous exercise that exhausts people; running is seen as the best example of cardio, but other examples include swimming and dancing. Cycling is a very fun form of cardio, as well. Cardio is great for improving cardiovascular health. For fitness, cardio is also well known for its ability to burn calories. It can also improve endurance and stamina, making it easier to perform daily tasks and other forms of exercise. However, cardio alone may not be enough to build significant muscle mass or improve strength.

HIIT is great for improving cardio. It is characterized by bursts of very hard exercise followed by a rest period before the next round. Of course, it's also known for burning calories and is perhaps the most efficient at doing so. As an added bonus, it builds muscle mass better than running. It can also be a time-efficient way to get in a good workout, considering that these exercises are completed in as little as 20-30 minutes. Despite all the upsides, HIIT can be very challenging and may not be suitable for individuals with certain health conditions or fitness levels. HIIT is not an accessible exercise for people who haven't consistently worked out in the past.

Weightlifting is a simple concept. It can be used in HIIT, but it also is often done slowly with higher weights. Weightlifting is a great way of becoming stronger while also increasing your muscle mass. Weightlifting can also help burn calories, but it's not as efficient as the other exercises. Most notably, weightlifting can cause injury to your muscles because it often involves hitting them with a lot of intense strain at once.

We, as the authors of this book, recommend running and doing so in proper form, while exercising with light weights. Cardio is one of the best ways to prevent heart disease and sustain connective tissue. Weightlifting is known to be bad for the heart and cholesterol in higher levels, and HIIT is known to induce injury (and it's a very difficult thing to do consistently). Lightweight training can help reinforce muscles (like the core, which is known to help sustain mobility in old age) without risking injury or potentially causing heart issues.

When exercising to lose weight, you need to sustain a caloric deficit, which means that you need to consistently burn more calories than you consume. Though that implies you need to eat less (and that is true), that doesn't mean that you should directly reduce your portions. If you're looking for a caloric deficit, you should refer to the nutrition section and see if you can reduce the poor macronutrients while sustaining the good ones.

In the following boxes on the next page, write out a workout plan for the next week and think about what you would work towards while following it.

Day	Exercise
Monday	
Tuesday	
Wednesday	
Thursday	

Friday	
Saturday	
Sunday	

Chapter 3: Sleep

Just about every adult knows the impossibility of completing a complicated task while exhausted. Sleep, as a subject, is known to be incredibly complicated and not fully understood, even by top scientists. What we confidently know is that sleep is necessary and that there are four stages of sleep. Beyond that, the consequences, both long and short of not getting enough sleep are very well-known.

The Stages of Sleep

Sleep is one of the most important things that we do daily (probably second only to drinking water). It is essential. While we sleep, our body undergoes a series of physiological changes that help us to rest, recover, and rejuvenate.

However, the process of sleep is much more complex than we might realize. There are four stages of sleep, each with its own unique characteristics and functions. In this chapter, we will delve deeper into the four stages of sleep and explore what happens to our bodies during each stage.

Stage 1

This stage is light, and it lasts for around 5-10 minutes. During this stage, our brainwave activity slows down, and our body relaxes. This is the only stage that we fully remember. It's the stage of sleep where we're drifting off into dreamland.

In stage 1 NREM, our heart rate slows down, our breathing becomes more regular, and our body temperature drops slightly. Our muscles also relax, but we may experience sudden muscle contractions. These jerks are a normal physiological response and are not harmful. In this stage, we may experience hypnagogic hallucinations, which are vivid and often bizarre sensory experiences that occur as we fall asleep. These hallucinations can involve any of the five senses and may include vivid colors, shapes, sounds, or smells.

Stage 2

The second stage of NREM lasts around 20-30 minutes. In this stage, our brainwave activity continues to slow down while we relax even further. Our heart rate and breathing continue to slow down, and our body temperature drops further.

Stage 3

This stage is "deep sleep." Deep sleep occurs within the first few hours of sleep and lasts for around 20-40 minutes. In this stage, our brainwave activity slows down even further. This stage is also known as slow-wave sleep.

During deep sleep, our breathing and heart rate reach their lowest levels, and our body temperature drops to its lowest point. Our muscles are completely relaxed, and it can be challenging to wake us up from this stage. Physical restoration is a crucial part of deep sleep. During this stage, your body performs its repairs. It replaces damaged tissues, helps your immune system, and builds up bones and muscles. Deep sleep is also known to help with memory consolidation and learning, though this assertion doesn't have too solid of evidence.

Stage 4: REM Sleep

REM sleep usually comes about after about 90 minutes of sleep, and you are usually in REM for 10-60 minutes. During REM, your brain is very active, even though the body is in a state of paralysis. REM occurs multiple times throughout the night, with each REM cycle lasting longer as the night progresses.

During REM sleep, the brain is engaged in a bunch of activities, including processing emotions, consolidating memories, and regulating mood. It is believed that the dreaming that occurs while in REM is a result of your brain processing and integrating various experiences and emotions from the previous day.

Knowing these stages and what they do for us, it's even more clear why sleep is so necessary. Sustaining your emotions, committing things to memory, and even repairing brain cells are tasks that you unknowingly complete while you're asleep!

If your sleep schedule is well-made, your REM should follow this graph created by the sleep foundation:[1]

---

[1] https://www.sleepfoundation.org/stages-of-sleep

Sleep Cycles Through the Night

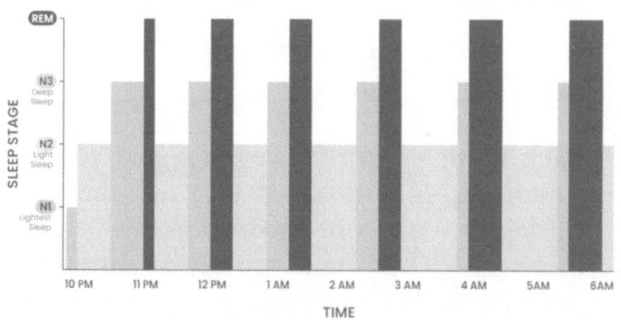

Think about what time you go to sleep and note how the REM time increases as the night goes on, which implies that (up to eight hours) your sleep becomes more and more valuable the longer that it goes on! How many hours do you sleep, and therefore, how many REM cycles do you get through nightly? Instead of generalizing, think about it in terms of days of the week and fill out the days in this chart:

Day	REM's
Monday	
Tuesday	
Wednesday	
Thursday	
Friday	
Saturday	
Sunday	

Deprivation

Deprivation of sleep can cause plenty of negative factors. To name a few:

1. Lack of sleep can cause impaired cognitive function, including decreased alertness, difficulty with concentration, and impaired memory. This can make it difficult to perform daily tasks and can increase the risk of accidents.

2. Sleep deprivation can cause changes in mood, including irritability, mood swings, and increased anxiety or depression. This is due in part to the disruption of the body's natural hormonal balance that occurs when sleep is insufficient.

3. Lack of sleep often means that your immune system doesn't receive the maintenance that it needs, meaning that you may be more susceptible to illness.

4. Sleep deprivation can cause physical fatigue, making it difficult to perform physical tasks.

5. Studies have shown that sleep deprivation can lead to increased appetite and cravings for fatty and unhealthy food, which often increase your chance of weight gain and obesity.

6. When you're tired, you're unable to react to things as quickly, which makes it harder for you to respond quickly to sudden events or changes in the environment. This can be particularly dangerous when driving or operating heavy machinery.

It can be argued easily that long-term consequences would come as products of these effects (e.g., you can't drive because you're exhausted, or you become sick and have to take a couple of days off work), but there are even more consequences to worry about when you skip out on sleep!

Of long-term consequences, there are two that are notably apparent and consequential:

1. Increased risk of chronic health conditions: Studies have shown that chronic sleep deprivation can increase the chances of contracting a number of chronic illnesses, which include depression, diabetes, and a variety of heart diseases. Over time, chronic sleep deprivation can lead to systemic inflammation, hormonal imbalances, and other physiological changes that can contribute to the development of these conditions.

2. Impaired cognitive function: Chronic sleep deprivation can also cause long-term impairments in cognitive function, including memory loss, decreased attention span, and impaired decision-making abilities.

Knowing that sleep deprivation can mess up your life in both the long and short-term, you're probably looking to fix or prevent it as soon as possible. As listed previously, one of the best ways to help yourself get some sleep is to develop a sleep routine. Let's do that! Create a four-step plan for the next time you sleep.

Step 1:

Step 2:

Step 3:

Step 4:

Now that you have a plan, think about the other pieces of advice you read and consider whether or not you applied them. Did you create a better sleep environment? Did you make sure that you didn't eat any heavy foods before sleeping?

Chapter 4: Mental Health

Mental health seems easy for some but unbelievably difficult for others. Generally, it's understood that, regardless of severity, everybody has had a run-in with poor mental health. Mental health is a clear marker of how long somebody will live.

While other chapters have covered specific topics and their solutions, the topic of mental health is a bit too severe and nuanced to even give a reasonable general opinion on specific illnesses. Instead, we're going to be covering common signs of those illnesses and general tips for improving one's mental health overall, regardless of specific illnesses!

Cultivating a Peaceful Mind

There are about ten different common suggestions for keeping your mind healthy. When thinking about these things, it is best to understand that this information is meant for everyone, and beyond mental health advice, every one of the pieces enumerated falls well under the guise of life advice. Here they are:

1. Practicing mindfulness is one of the most important actions you can take to cultivate better mental health. Mindfulness is the practice of being present and fully engaged in the moment.

It involves being fully aware of what you are thinking, feeling, and doing, all of which you are likely not fully aware of. Mindfulness can be exercised through a variety of actions. At some points, mindfulness doesn't require any action at all— all you have to do is think: "How do I feel at this point of the day? Why do I feel this way? Why am I thinking about these things, and how do they deeply make me feel?"

Furthermore, you can practice mindfulness through meditation— both in the practice of letting your thoughts flow freely and through thinking deeply about certain concepts that have been elusive or challenging for you. One of the best forms of mindfulness is simply deep breathing. Deep breathing causes you to stop and remove yourself from situations temporarily, which can give you a new perspective.

2. We've covered why sleep is so essential. Sleep, beyond many things, is crucial for maintaining a healthy mind. You're not your best when you're tired. Try to follow our previous sleep advice in order to help improve the quality of your sleep!

3. Keeping a diet that helps your brain establish certain hormones, such as the micronutrients (e.g., zinc and its role in aiding in the production of hormones) previously mentioned. Variety is also a good habit for your diet because even when it seems like you're hitting all of the recommended daily intakes, you might be missing something! Worst case, you're missing one or two of your micronutrients for a day (which would not be enough missed in order to cultivate a deficiency).

4. Positive relationships and a healthy mind go one-to-one. When you have people that support you and make you happy, you're going to feel better! Furthermore, social validation is a necessary thing for most people— and that's alright! Spend time with people who support and uplift you. Avoid toxic relationships that drain

your energy and people who leave you feeling stressed and anxious.

5. Exercise is known to be a necessary thing for mental health. Elevating your heart rate (even infrequently) throughout the week has numerous benefits for both the body and mind. Regular exercise is known to reduce stress, improve mood, boost self-esteem, and even help you think more clearly.

6. Engaging in hobbies and activities you enjoy helps you clear your mind and creates an environment where you're consistently happy. Take time each week to engage in hobbies or activities that you enjoy.

7. Practicing gratitude is a great way to keep your head healthy! Gratitude is the practice of appreciating the things that are nice in your life instead of ruminating over shortcomings. Cultivating a sense of gratitude can help improve mood, increase resilience, and enhance overall well-being. Take time each day to reflect on the things you are grateful for.

8. Stress is a normal part of life, and accepting it as something inevitable can be healthy in and of itself. But excessive stress is known to be very bad for you— it

raises your blood pressure, makes it harder to think clearly, and generally just makes you unhappy. Learn to manage stress through different relaxation techniques, which can be similar to those of mindfulness.

9. Learning new things can help keep your mind active. When you're thinking and feeling successful about your new knowledge, you're going to feel happier! Furthermore, helping keep your mind active is one of the best ways. Try to take a class or learn a new language. Even picking up a hobby and learning about it can help you keep your mind active and growing. On top of the benefits of learning that we've already listed, learning new things also helps you grow as a person!

10. Seek professional help if needed. If you feel like your struggle with mental health is especially severe or insurmountable, then there is no answer beyond a mental health profession!

We would like to emphasize the tenth step. If you are struggling with your mental health, these steps may be helpful, but they are far from a solution. The only solution anyone should follow is one from a mental health professional who is giving it to them directly. There are no substitutions.

Specific Mental illnesses

Depression

Depression is perhaps the most talked about mental illness. Often, it is conflated with other illnesses, but that is also because it is symptomatic of many greater issues (not to assert, that is, that depression could be identified as a "lesser" issue at all).

Depression is a disorder that causes despair. Despair is a feeling of discontent, unhappiness, or a general loss of hope. Beyond just the feelings (though please don't reduce the emotional turmoil of depression— it is severe), there are physical reactions that your body has to the illness. These include changes in appetite and sleep patterns. You may also experience unexplained aches and pains.

Symptoms of Depression:

The most obvious symptom of depression is a constant feeling of sadness that can't be remedied.

Depression can cause you to lose interest in activities that you used to enjoy, such as hobbies, socializing, or spending time with loved ones.

People with depression often report feeling tired and lacking in energy, even after getting enough sleep.

Depression often causes large changes in appetite, resulting in fluctuations in one's figure— be it weight gain or weight loss, both of which are known to further the issues of depression.

Depression can make you irritable, especially when the issue is present in children and adolescents. This is characteristic of the symptom of mental exhaustion, especially when one's mood is unstable.

People with depression may have difficulty concentrating. Making decisions or remembering details are often results of the difficulty with concentration that people have, as well as mental exhaustion.

Depression can cause negative self-talk, such as feelings of guilt, worthlessness, or hopelessness.

Depression can cause problems physically, such as unexplained soreness, headaches, or digestive issues.

Depression can lead to thoughts of suicide or self-harm. If you or someone you know is experiencing suicidal thoughts, seek help immediately.

Please remember that a symptom is almost never universal, regardless of an illness!

Depression comes in a wide variety of forms, and besides the symptoms, understanding the different forms and causes of depression can help you take action before it takes full swing:

We've compiled a list and some brief explanations of each of the major forms of depression.

MDD stands for major depressive disorder. MDD is the best known and most common form of depression. When you think of depression, you're probably also thinking of MDD. Symptoms of MDD include exhaustion, feelings of despair, a loss of love in things that you were once passionate about, and general sadness. MDD can interfere with daily life, and it may require treatment to manage symptoms.

Persistent depressive disorder, or PDD, is a milder form of depression that lasts for at least two years. It is characterized by symptoms similar to MDD, and it can interfere with daily life.

SAD Stands for seasonal affective disorder/depression. It often occurs during months when there is less visible sunlight, but it is not excluded to the Winter months, and it depends on the individual.

PPD stands for postpartum depression. It is a type of depression that occurs after childbirth. The usual symptoms of depression, but symptoms of anxiety are more common, and it's common that a mother will have difficulty bonding with the baby.

Anxiety

Anxiety is a common mental illness, but it is very often misunderstood. Anxiety is characterized by feelings of fear or uneasiness that don't properly or logically match the present threat. Beyond emotions, anxiety can cause symptoms such as an increased heartbeat, excessive sweating, shaking, and trouble breathing. Anxiety can also cause avoidance of situations or activities that trigger the symptoms, which can significantly impact daily life.

Types of Anxiety:

Anxiety comes in plenty of different forms, each with its own problems and causes.

Generalized Anxiety Disorder, or GAD, is known by the symptoms of persistent and excessive worry about a variety of topics. These topics include health, finances, and relationships. People with GAD may feel restless or fatigued. Many people with GAD have difficulty concentrating.

Panic Disorder is known by abrupt and powerful episodes of fear. Physical symptoms like a rapid heartbeat, sweating, and shortness of breath are known to be characteristic of this form of anxiety.

Social Anxiety Disorder, or SAD, is demonstrated by a severe fear of social situations, specifically public speaking or meeting new people. Panic attacks and severe isolation aren't rare among people with social anxiety disorder. Everyone believes to have a certain level of social anxiety, so many often assume that they have this disorder without proper research.

Specific phobias are characterized by an intense fear and avoidant behavior of a specific object or situation. Examples of specific phobias include heights, spiders, or flying.

Obsessive-Compulsive Disorder, or OCD, is known for intrusive, unwanted compulsions. Many people are facetious regarding OCD, but many of the compulsive behaviors have been severely harmful to individuals.

Post-Traumatic Stress Disorder, or PTSD, is known by the intense anxiety and intrusive memories or flashbacks that people experience after experiencing or witnessing a traumatic event, usually a natural disaster or violent crime.

Treatment for Anxiety:

Anxiety doesn't simply mean doom; there are treatments and solutions! The most common treatments for anxiety include medication, psychotherapy, or a combination of the two.

Several types of medication can be used to treat anxiety, including antidepressants, benzodiazepines, and beta-blockers. These medications can help to reduce the physical symptoms of anxiety and improve mood.

Anxiety disorders can also be treated by a special method of therapy known as Cognitive

Behavioral Therapy. CBT is useful mostly in helping people become aware of thought and behavioral patterns that are destructive to their mental health. It is known as a practice of mindfulness, though it has clinical guidance to make sure that the patient is following the right path.

Exposure therapy is often used to treat specific phobias and PTSD. Exposure therapy works by gradually exposing the person to what creates anxiety or episodes, be it an object or situation in which the source of anxiety is introduced in a controlled environment.

Bipolar Disorder

Bipolar disorder is another mental illness that is well-known but not understood very well by most people. This is perhaps due to the misattribution of bipolar disorder to people who frequently have mood swings or change their minds.

Bipolar disorder is understood and seen by alternating episodes of depression and mania. During a manic episode, you may experience an elevated or irritable mood, increased energy, and a decreased need for sleep. This is looked at as an episode of insanity, though it's a harmful mischaracterization. During a depressive episode, you likely experience feelings of sadness and hopelessness. Because of these symptoms, a loss of interest is often present.

Bipolar disorder is known to affect an estimated 1-3% of people all over the world.

There are three types of this disorder: I, II, and Cyclothymic. There are other untitled and unspecified forms of bipolar disorders. Bipolar I disorder is the most severe form of the illness. Bipolar I is characterized by at least one manic episode that lasts for at least a week or that requires hospitalization. Bipolar II is known for hypomania episodes, which are still manic episodes, but they're less severe than manic episodes (do not be misled to think that they aren't too severe), as well as at least one major depressive episode.

We're not sure of the exact causes of bipolar disorder. The causes are believed to be caused by a mix of genetics, early lifestyle, and neurological factors. Bipolar disorder is common in families. There are also certain genes that have been linked to the illness. Environmental factors may also play a role in triggering bipolar episodes.

There are also mixed episodes, which may include symptoms of both mania and depression.

The diagnosis of bipolar disorder is not taken lightly. It is always carried out by an experienced medical professional who reviews various records, which include a review of medical history. They also look deeply at the symptoms and the patient's family history. There are no specific laboratory tests or imaging studies that can diagnose bipolar disorder, but some lab tests are used to make sure that the disorder is not actually another disease that is being confused with bipolar disorder.

The treatment of bipolar disorder is two-pronged and includes the application of therapy and the prescription of medicine that is specific to the individual. Medications such as mood stabilizers and antipsychotics are common in the treatment, and antidepressants may be used to manage symptoms of bipolar disorder. Therapy, such as cognitive-behavioral therapy, may be helpful in managing symptoms and improving quality of life.

Living with bipolar disorder can be challenging, but with proper treatment as well as family and loved ones that are supporting the afflicted, plenty of people have been able to reduce the complications that come with the disease and live happy, full lives. It's crucial that someone who was diagnosed with bipolar disorder not only meets with a mental health expert but works closely with them frequently so that they can plan a treatment that is suited for their specific needs and situation.

Conclusion on Disorders

This mantra cannot be repeated enough: If you are seeking a solution to an ongoing mental health crisis, it is not present in this book. The only solution that should be sought after is a mental health professional.

If you feel like the descriptions of these mental illnesses fit you well, then there is a chance that the illness itself describes you. Interpreting one of the descriptions as descriptive of yourself, however, does not mean that you have the illness. Ideas are misinterpreted frequently, and so is the self. If you feel like one of these illnesses fits you, we advise you to visit a mental health professional and seek a diagnosis before taking action.

The best way to habitual good mental health (beyond following the previously described steps to cultivating a healthy mind) is to log your feelings and daily actions and then look back on them to better understand how you feel at different times.

Chapter 5: Chronic Illnesses

When thinking about how one could live as long as possible, few things come to mind, as much as chronic illnesses and the threats that they pose against longevity. In this chapter, we're going to be explaining the different kinds of chronic illnesses by splitting them up into the categories: Chronic illnesses of the mind, Chronic illnesses of the organs (specifically of the kidneys, liver, and other parts of the digestive system), and Chronic skeletal/nervous illnesses. Furthermore, in the interest of outliving, the illnesses being described are going to be ones that are mainly caused by old age.

Chronic Illnesses of the Mind

We're only going to talk about one chronic illness of the mind in this chapter. Other chronic illnesses of the mind were covered in the "Mental Health" chapter.

Though we're categorizing it into one disease, don't be confused to think that dementia is a disease, as it is often conflated with Alzheimer's, a disease of which dementia is symptomatic.

Dementia

Dementia isn't a specific disease. It's a condition that is used to describe a decline in cognitive ability, especially in old age. Dementia is often associated with aging and can cause memory loss, confusion, but most characteristically and notably: difficulty with daily activities. Dementia affects about 50 million people worldwide. Excelling beyond population growth, that number is expected to triple by 2050. Dementia is a major public health concern that may soon have a significant impact on both individuals and society.

Alzheimer's is the most attributed disease that is labeled as dementia. It makes up around 61-80% of all dementia cases. Vascular dementia, one of many forms of dementia, is caused when there isn't proper blood flow to the brain.

Symptoms of dementia can change based on the individual. However, there are some common symptoms, including:

Memory loss is characteristic of dementia. Many people have no concept of dementia or Alzheimer's beyond memory loss. That's not for a bad reason; memory loss is one of the most common symptoms of dementia, especially at the beginning of the disease's onset. People with dementia may have difficulty remembering events, people's names, or information that is necessary in order to function on a daily basis.

Dementia can affect a person's ability to speak and understand language. Often, a person will struggle to find the right words or have trouble following a conversation.

Dementia inevitably causes difficulty with daily activities. As dementia progresses, people may struggle with daily activities such as dressing, bathing, and cooking.

People with dementia may experience changes in their personality, such as becoming more withdrawn, irritable, or aggressive. Personality changes are one of the most obvious indicators of early dementia.

Dementia can cause confusion and disorientation, which makes it once again difficult to complete daily and necessary activities.

Difficulty with spatial awareness: Some types of dementia can cause problems with spatial awareness, which make it hard to understand distance or navigate.

Many assume that dementia will slowly creep up on someone, but that's not always the case— the onset of dementia can happen both quickly and slowly, and its progression is not set to a certain pace either; the progression of dementia can vary suddenly (for the better or worse) for little-to-no apparent reason. Some people have experienced a rapid decline, while others may have worked through a more gradual decline over several years. There is no cure for dementia, and treatment options are limited. Despite this, there are treatments that are able to make the symptoms less severe while increasing the quality of life as the disease progresses.

Perhaps the most important thing to understand about dementia is that its detection is crucial. Early detection means early treatment and preparation, which can make all the difference. If you or a loved one are undergoing anything similar to these symptoms, please receive medical attention promptly. A healthcare provider can perform a variety of tests and assessments to determine the cause of symptoms, and then they can help develop a treatment plan.

Managing symptoms is important. Not only does it help keep one's mind intact, but it prevents the feeling of hopelessness after diagnosis. Beyond healthcare, individual management of symptoms includes:

Regular exercise can help improve overall health and thinking. Many people with dementia become sedentary, which is harmful to their mental and physical health. It's important to counteract that.

A changing diet that does not lack whole grains and necessary micronutrients is very important.

Furthermore, variety can help stimulate one's mind without overwhelming them.

Engaging with other people socially is a good way to prevent or manage symptoms of dementia. When you're engaging with other people, your brain is working in special and specific ways.

Engaging in mentally stimulating activities, such as puzzles or games, can help improve cognitive function. Just try to keep your mind active!

Support groups are a great way to work through the symptoms of dementia. Not only do they make your brain more active, but support groups allow you to see the disease from a new, active perspective that is beyond yourself.

Dementia is one of the hardest conditions to deal with, especially for those who are close to someone affected by the disease. With early detection and management, improving quality of life is absolutely possible! Furthermore, one could maintain independence for as long as possible, and for the loved ones, it helps them prepare for what is to come.

Chronic Organ Illnesses

As people age, their organs and bodies become more susceptible to chronic illnesses. There are several chronic illnesses that are especially common in older people that affect the organs, including the heart, lungs, and kidneys.

Heart disease is a pretty complicated thing. It's the leading cause of death in America, with over 600,000 deaths each year, and there is a myriad of ongoing debates as to who is to blame. Because there are so many different forms of heart disease and they cause so much death, we're only going to focus on one type so that we can focus your attention and our energy on making sure that coronary heart disease is well understood.

Of various heart diseases, coronary heart disease is the most common. Coronary artery disease occurs when the blood vessels that bring oxygen and nutrients to your heart become narrow or clogged up. The clogged or tiny blood vessels can lead to chest pain or discomfort, shortness of breath, and a variety of other (potentially fatal) symptoms. Heart failure occurs when your heart can't effectively pump blood anymore. Minor heart failure (a struggling heart) can lead to fatigue and shortness of breath, as well as worse issues in the future. Arrhythmias, or abnormal heart rhythms, can cause palpitations and dizziness.

High blood pressure and high cholesterol are both severe risk factors for heart disease. Smoking, diabetes, and a history of heart disease in your family are other predictors of heart disease. Changes in lifestyle, like eating well, regular exercise, and avoiding tobacco, can help lower your chances of contracting heart disease. Treatment options for heart disease may include medications, lifestyle changes, and in some cases, surgery.

COPD is a chronic lung disease. COPD causes airflow obstruction, and because of that, it can be difficult to breathe for victims of COPD. It is another leading cause of death worldwide and is especially common in older adults. Bronchitis and emphysema are the two main types of COPD.

Emphysema is characterized by damage to the little bags that hold air in your lungs, while chronic bronchitis is a chronic cough and excessive production of mucus.

Symptoms of COPD include shortness of breath, coughing, and wheezing. These symptoms, as you can imagine, will significantly impact daily life and lead to decreased quality of life, as well as byproducts of the inability to be as physically active as you usually are.

Smoking and exposure to air pollution or occupational dust are the main risk factors for COPD— try to breathe clean air! A family history of COPD can also be a strong predictor. Treatment options for COPD often include medications, pulmonary rehabilitation (therapy for your respiratory), and oxygen therapy. Lifestyle changes such as quitting smoking and avoiding triggers such as air pollution can also help manage symptoms.

Chronic kidney disease (CKD) is characterized by a progressive failure of the kidneys. It's a common condition among older people and leads to serious complications like kidney failure and cardiovascular disease.

CKD is usually asymptomatic in its early stages, which makes it so that it sneaks up on a lot of people! As the disease progresses, symptoms often include fatigue, swelling, and changes in your urine.

Treatment options for CKD may include medications, maintaining a healthy diet, and regular exercise. Dialysis or kidney transplants are necessary in some cases. Early detection and management of CKD are essential to prevent complications and maintain kidney function.

Chronic Bone and Nervous Illnesses

Osteoporosis affects your bones and makes them weak and brittle. Osteoporosis is especially common among older adults, specifically women who have gone through menopause.

Osteoporosis occurs when the body loses bone mass faster than it can replace it, leading to weak and fragile bones. The condition can occur without symptoms, making it difficult to detect until something bad— like a fracture— happens. Fractures that are caused by osteoporosis occur most often in places with a lot of use, like the wrist, spine, and hip.

Prevention and management of osteoporosis involve a combination of lifestyle changes and medical interventions. Diets that have plenty of calcium and vitamin D are one of the best methods of prevention. Furthermore, engaging in regular exercise is one of the easiest and most popular recommendations. Avoiding tobacco and excessive alcohol intake also help reduce the risk of osteoporosis. Medications such as bisphosphonates and denosumab may also be prescribed to help slow bone loss and reduce the risk of fractures.

Diagnosis of osteoporosis is typically made through a bone density test, which measures the amount of bone marrow in various areas of the body. The test is painless and noninvasive and can help detect osteoporosis before a fracture occurs. Treatment may include lifestyle changes, medication, and fall prevention strategies to reduce the risk of fractures.

Complications of osteoporosis can be severe, especially if a fracture occurs in the hip or spine, which is not only more likely with the disease but significantly more severe. Hip fractures significantly damage mobility and independence, and spinal fractures can cause chronic pain and deformities if the healing process isn't ideal. Complications can be reduced through early detection and management of osteoporosis.

Arthritis is a condition that affects the joints, causing pain, swelling, and stiffness. There are over 100 different forms of the disease, but the two most prevalent forms are rheumatoid arthritis and osteoarthritis.

Rheumatoid arthritis is a disease where the body progressively tears down the tissue that cushions and protects joints, which, like osteoarthritis, causes inflammation and damage (and that horrible *grinding*). This can lead to joint deformities and even a complete loss of function.

Osteoarthritis is a degenerative disease in the joints that occurs when the cartilage that pads the ends of the bones wear down over time. This can lead to bone-on-bone contact and grinding, causing pain and inflammation. Osteoarthritis most commonly affects the hands, hips, and knees.

Rheumatoid arthritis most commonly affects the hands and feet. Risk factors for arthritis include age and family history, while joint injuries, obesity, and certain medical conditions such as diabetes and gout are also often considered.

Although a cure for arthritis is unknown, early diagnosis and treatment can ease pain and help with quality of life. If you're having joint pain or stiffness that goes on for more than a couple of weeks, it's important to talk to a professional.

Parkinson's is a disease in your brain that makes precise movement progressively difficult. Progressive, meaning that it only gets worse as it goes on. Parkinson's comes about when the production of dopamine in the brain slowly degenerates. This causes a lower amount of dopamine, which is a neurotransmitter that is essential for smooth and coordinated movements.

Symptoms of Parkinson's include shaking, rigidity, and slowness of movement. As a product, difficulty with balance and coordination will also happen inevitably. Other symptoms include changes in speech and handwriting, depression and anxiety, as well as difficulty processing complex ideas or thoughts.

No cure is known for Parkinson's, but there is medication. Levodopa is the most common medication for Parkinson's disease; it helps to replace the dopamine that is lacking in the brain. Other medications are also often needed in order to manage specific symptoms, specifically tremors or sleep disturbances.

With medication, doctors often prescribe physical therapy and exercise, as they can also be beneficial for people with Parkinson's disease. These forms of therapy can help improve flexibility, balance, and coordination, which (most importantly) will reduce the risk of falls.

The research for the treatment and source of Parkinson's is ongoing. Even though the exact cause of the disease is not fully understood, genetics and environmental factors are assumed to play a role. Many studies suggest that exposure to certain toxins may increase the risk of developing Parkinson's disease.

Conclusion

Peter Attia's life advice is perennially applicable and intelligent. Understanding this information is a very important task for anybody who wants to live a long life. While *knowing* the information is half the battle, it's only half the battle. Once we've learned everything that there is to learn, we need to apply it consistently. This book's goal was not only to inform you, the reader, about the different issues of sleep, exercise, mental health, nutrition, and illness but to help you internalize that information and apply it to yourself in ways that make a change in your life!

Taking away these different ideas is crucial for living long! Think about the different things that you knew before reading this book and compare them to what you know now. What did you know that was reinforced here? What did you think that you knew before being proven wrong? What were a few things that were completely new to you as you read through this book?

Our advice after reading this book is to do it again. Don't read this and check it off your list of things that you meant to do— live by this book. Reread this book slowly, applying the advice from each section until you're certain that it is something set in your life. Furthermore, please understand that applying all of the advice in this book is nearly impossible. If you were to become a fully centered, well-read, athletic person with an incredible diet, then great job! However, as humans, creating habits (especially ones that don't especially feel good, such as cutting out sugary foods or never going to bed late) is one of the hardest things that we work on for the entirety of our lives. Being human is synonymous with being imperfect.

All this to say: If you are having a hard time committing to a habit, don't beat yourself up! "If at first you don't succeed, you're in good company"— Chris Arnold. The only time that you fail at applying this advice is when you stop trying to do so!

Finally: This is not professional advice. This advice is not suited to you. This information is intentionally general, but despite that, this information (as well as just about any other piece of advice that is worth reading) does not apply to everybody.

Manufactured by Amazon.ca
Bolton, ON